CIRCULAR LETTER

FROM

HON. JOHN M. BRIGHT,

TO THE CITIZENS

OF THE

4TH CONGRESSIONAL DISTRICT,

STATE OF TENNESSEE.

FAYETTEVILLE, TENN.:
THE FAYETTEVILLE EXPRESS PRINT.
1873.

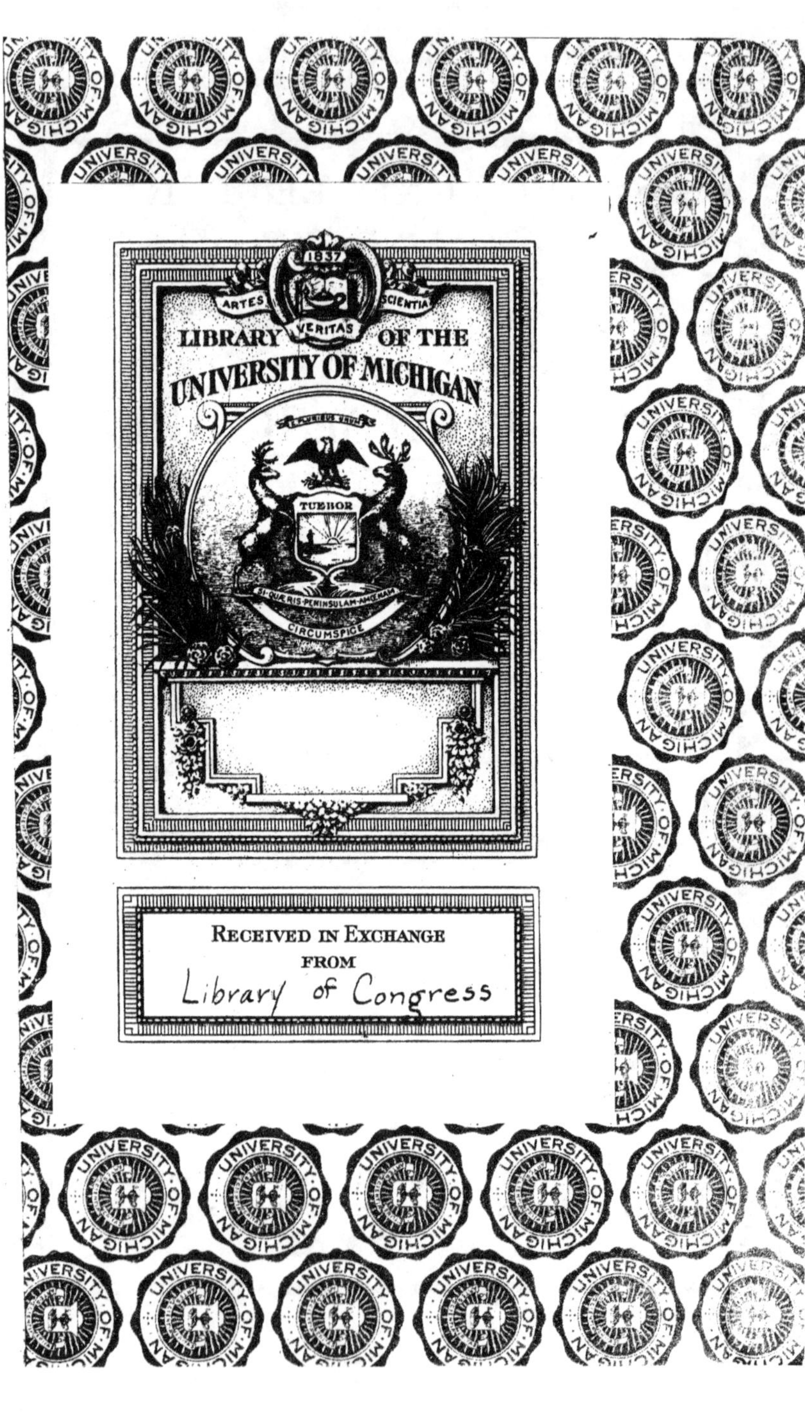
1837
ARTES
SCIENTIA
VERITAS
LIBRARY OF THE
UNIVERSITY OF MICHIGAN
TUEBOR
SI QUÆRIS PENINSULAM AMŒNAM
CIRCUMSPICE
RECEIVED IN EXCHANGE
FROM
Library of Congress

CIRCULAR LETTER

FROM

HON. JOHN M. BRIGHT,

TO

The Citizens of the Fourth Congressional District, State of Tennessee.

A SENSE of duty to you, as well as to myself, induces me to make a communication to you, with respect to the recent salary bill, which increased the pay of the President and Vice-President, Cabinet officers and clerks in their different departments, Judges of the Supreme Court, members of Congress, clerks of the Senate and House of Representatives, and other employes of the Government.

I have nothing political to conceal from you. You are entitled to an account of my stewardship, and it is my duty to spread the record of it before you.

In times of great popular ferment, it was to be expected that many errors, perversions, and misrepresentations should be disseminated.

Under such circumstances, the public mind is inflamed, and abused by being fed on distorted information which has been driveled out to it from hand to hand, perhaps to the fortieth degree.

My own action has been the subject of misrepresentations which, together with a call from some of my constituents, must furnish my apology for this communication.

In an editorial of the New York Sun, commenting on the salary bill, in its issue of 27th August, 1873, is the following statement:

"In the final test vote in the House, on the 1st of March last, the following members then, or since, chosen to the Forty-third Congress recorded themselves thus"—and amongst the Democrats placed under the head of "absent or dodging," my name is recorded.

The following is an extract from the Murfreesboro News, of August 15, 1873:

"In a complete list of the Senators and Representatives who voted for and against the back salary fraud, published in the New York Tribune, we find that Hon. John M. Bright, the member from this district, is reported to have voted one time for it, twice against it, and was absent, or refused to vote five times."

In the Murfreesboro Monitor, of August 28, 1873, I find the following:

"Editors Monitor:—It is my understanding that Hon. John M. Bright opposed the salary bill, passed at the last session of Congress. Upon what ground did he base his opposition? If so, what does he intend to do with it? Is the bill constitutional? By answering the above, you will much oblige,

Constituent."

The statements in the Sun and Tribune—assuming that the News has correctly extracted from the Tribune—are grossly perversive of the facts. I did not "dodge" the "final" vote, nor did I vote for the salary bill which became the law—nor did I vote for any other bill to increase the pay of members of Congress. I was opposed to it from the beginning to the ending—I voted against the first bill and voted against the last. In the intermediate stages of the question, my opposition to it was so marked by votes and declarations, that no one, after investigation, who regards the truth of history, could believe that I favored the passage of the bill, or had occasion to "dodge" the responsibility of a vote after having been so fully committed against it. It is true that I did not vote on several occasions when the bill was before the House, but these failures to vote were when I was paired off with another, or on parliamentary questions not going to the merit—except in the single instance I did not vote on what is known as the Sargeant amendment, which was entirely a different thing from the Butler amendment, which became the law.

But I will allude to these votes and omissions to vote more specifically in the following legislative narratives, to which I invite your careful attention.

The salary bill presents two aspects for your consideration. One is legislative, and the other is personal.

LEGISLATIVE ACTION ON THE BILL.

On the 7th of February, 1873, Mr. Butler, of Massachusetts, from the House Judiciary Committee, reported the salary bill, known as the Butler bill, which was ordered to be printed and recommitted to the same committee. (Globe, part 2, p. 1196—42d Congress.)

On the 10th of the same month, Mr. Butler introduced a resolution directing the Committee on Appropriations to include his salary bill in the miscellaneous appropriation bill for the consideration of the committee of the whole House, and moved a suspension of the rules to put it on its passage. On a call of the ayes and noes, I voted against this resolution—the vote standing yeas 81, nays 120—not voting 39. (Globe, part 2, p. 1234.)

This vote was so decided against even the consideration of the bill, that I supposed it was the end of it. But I was mistaken. It was destined to re-appear with greater force at another time.

On the 3d of December, 1872, the Executive, Legislative, and Judiciary appropriation bill was introduced into the House.

On the 15th of January, 1873, this bill passed the House with a provision increasing the pay of sundry clerks and officers of the House and interior department of the Government. But it contained no provision to increase the pay of the President and members of Congress.

On the 16th of January, this bill was transmitted to the Senate, and, on the 30th of January, it passed the Senate with sundry amendments—the Senate striking out the increased pay of the officers of the House and increasing the pay of different officers of the Senate. (Globe, part 2, pp. 964–967.

On the 31st of January, the Senate returned the bill to the House as amended, and the House ordered the amendments to be printed, and referred to the Committee on Appropriations. (Globe, part 2, p. 1012.)

On the 24th of February, the committee made their report to the House, recommending an increase of the pay of clerks and other officers of the House, to make them equal in compensation to the same grade of officers in the Senate. (Globe, part 3, pp. 1670–1671.)

So far, the House and Senate had been at disagreement in relation to the compensation of the officers of the respective bodies.

The House resolved itself into the Committee of the Whole for the purpose of considering the report of the committee—whereupon Mr. Butler, of Massachusetts, moved to amend the amendment reported from the Committee of the Whole, by substituting the salary bill previously reported from the Judiciary Committee and rejected by the House. (Globe, part 3, pp. 1671–2.)

Mr. Butler's amendment was now carried on a division of the Committee of the Whole, by a vote of 81 ayes and 66 nays. (Globe, part 3, p. 1678.) It is my recollection that I was present, and voted in the negative, though I cannot verify the vote by record, as the "yeas" and "nays" are never ordered in the Committee of the Whole. The Legislative, Executive, and Judiciary bill, as amended, was now reported to the House, with a recommendation that it do pass. The previous question was moved and ordered upon the Butler amendment to the Senate amendment, and the "yeas" and "nays" being ordered, the vote stood: yeas 69, nays 121, not voting 50.

I did not vote at this time for the reason given at the time. During the roll call, the following announcements were made:

"Mr. Bright. On this question, I am paired with the gentleman from New York (Mr. Clark.) If he were present he would vote 'aye' while I should vote 'no.' (Globe, part 3, p. 1926.) Just here a word of explanation: I do not approve of the Congressional custom of pairing; but it has been too long established for me to correct. It does not change the result of the vote; and, by Congressional construction, the pairing members are considered as voting one for, and the other against, the question. To resume the narrative: The vote of the House against the Butler amendment to the Senate amendment seemed so decided, that Mr. Butler and his friends seemed to despair of its passage in the House. Mr. Butler had moved to reconsider the vote rejecting his amendment, and Mr. Farnsworth had moved to lay this last motion on the table. Mr. Butler now asked permission of the House to say: 'We are in such a position that unless we pass it in this form we cannot get any action. If we pass it, we can have the judgment of the Senate upon it. If they are against it, there is an end of the matter, and then it will go to a Committee of Conference, and they can agree and put the provision in such form as they think right. Then, it will come back to the House, and a majority of the House will have the control of the matter as they have now. Otherwise, it is a simple vote to put this case out of jurisdiction of the House and the Senate. This is why I moved to reconsider, in order that we may bring the minds of the two bodies to operate on the same proposition. I do not care whether the amount be fixed at $7,500, or $6,500, or $6,000, as some gentlemen have indicated; but I think there ought to be some increase to meet what is an actual reduction in our pay.'"

"Mr. Sargent. I suggest to the gentleman that he make it $6,500, and cut off all mileage and allowances."

"Mr. Butler. I will agree to an amendment which shall provide that this shall be the salary with actual expenses of travel."

"Mr. Sargent. I do not want actual expenses at all." (Globe, part 3, p. 1976.)

The vote was taken on Mr. Farnsworth's motion to lay on the table, which motion failed—yeas 66, nays 105, not voting 69. I was still paired with Mr. Clark, of New York, and did not vote on this question, but announced that I would vote "aye" if he were present. (Globe, part 3, p. 1977.) The question recurred on the motion to reconsider, and the vote stood: yeas 104, nays 79, not voting 57.

I did not vote on this question. The reason why I did not, I do not now remember. But I surely did not mean to "dodge" the question, as I was already fully committed against the bill, both by vote and declarations; and more especially as it was a parliamentary question to bring the matter before the House again, and not on its final passage.

Mr. Butler now moved to reconsider the vote by which the previous question was ordered, and it was agreed to without a call of yeas and nays. This brought the Senate amendment again before the House for amendment. Whereupon, Mr. Sargent moved to strike out of the Butler amendment $7,500, the proposed annual salary of members of Congress and their traveling expenses, and insert in lieu thereof: "Shall receive $6,500 per annum each; and this shall be in lieu of any other pay or any allowance for mileage, newspapers, or stationery." He called the previous question, which was ordered, and the vote was instantly thrust upon the House without explanation or debate. The House refused to order the yeas and nays, and the amendment of Mr. Sargent was agreed to.

The question then recurred on the agreement to the amendment as amended on motion of Mr. Sargent. The yeas and nays being ordered, the vote stood: yeas 100, nays 97, not voting 43. (Globe, part 3, p. 1977.)

I did not vote on this question, and it is the only one directly involving the merits, on which I did not vote, or declare how I would have voted, but for being paired. This omission, I am free to admit, requires explanation. There were two reasons, whether good or not, why I did not vote on this question: One, for the want of time to investigate the true construction and effect of the Sargent amendment and the difference in the pay to members of Congress between the amount allowed by the previous law: the other, that it was understood not to be a final vote, as Mr. Butler had previously declared that it was intended to go before the Committee of Conference of the two Houses, on whose report the final vote was to be taken. Upon investigation, I found this approximate result:

Under the previous law, annual salary	$5,000
Average mileage	900
Stationery, newspapers, and boxes	200
Free postage	400
	$6,500

In this aspect, the pay under the Sargent amendmendment would have been the same as the previous law to the people, but different in adjustment amongst the members. If this had been all, there would have been no clamor against it, if it had become the law; but I found, upon examination, that it was subject to insuperable objections which, had they been present to my mind, would have induced me to vote against it all the time. If I had voted for or against it, or any other proposition, it would have been my duty and my privilege, if I found that I was in error, to correct such error in a subsequent vote. But I was not mistaken in supposing that it was not the final vote. The real "tug of war" was yet to come. The disagreement of the two Houses resulted in the Conference Committee, as predicted. This committee agreed upon a report in which they rejected the Sargent amendment, and restored the Butler amendment. The final vote was taken on the conference report, on the 3d of March, the day before Congress adjourned, when I was present and deliberately recorded my vote against the whole Legislative, Executive, and Judiciary bill, because it contained the salary amendment. (Globe, part 3, p. 2105.)

The following is a substantial history of the legislation on the salary bill in the House of Representatives. If the perusal of the details have been a trial to your patience, I must plead justification in the great interest which the people have taken in the question, and to give the facts in their proper connection for their better understanding. So you will see that I was opposed to the passage of the law from the first to the last; did not aid in its passage, and in no just sense can be held responsible for its consequences. Six more negative votes would have defeated it on its final passage in the House; and after it passed the House, it might have been defeated in the Senate, and after it passed both Houses, the

President might have killed it with his veto. It never could have become a law except by the sanction of the President, or over his veto.

I am not, therefore, subject to the charge of voting to put money in my own pocket, or otherwise aiding in the passage of the law. There is no legislative power to compel a restitution from members whose term expired with the Forty-second Congress; but it seems that the rational way of correcting the evil of the future is by the repeal of the law.

This was the course pursued as to the obnoxious compensation bill of 1816.

PERSONAL ASPECT.

The application of the law to the members of Congress, after its passage, is broadly distinguishable from its legislative aspect.

In answer to the communication in the Monitor, in relation to the increase of the President's salary, I would say that, in my opinion, it was a violation of the spirit and reason of the Constitution, if not of the letter.

The Constitution declares that he "shall, at stated times, receive for his services a compensation which shall neither be increased nor diminished during the period for which he shall have been elected."

The object of this clause in giving a fixed salary was to make the President independent of Congress, and to put it out of the power of Congress to influence his action on legislation; or, as better expressed by Justice Story, so that Congress could "neither weaken his fortitude by operating on his necessities, nor corrupt his integrity by appealing to his avarice." (Story on Constitution, section 1486. 1 Kent, lecture 13, p. 263. Federalist, No. 73.)

It is unnecessary for me to argue that the increase of the President's salary did not make a powerful "appeal to his avarice" to approve the bill, and that the bill would not operate for his benefit, even though it was for his second term.

But the Constitution, as to the pay of members of Congress, is different from the provisions relating to the President's salary. It says: "The Senators and Representatives shall receive a compensation for their services, to be ascertained by law, and paid out of the treasury of the United States." This is all it says on the subject—nothing said about its being "increased or diminished" during the period for which he (or they) shall have been elected.

In passing, I would remark, that I do not agree with Senator Carpenter that the member, to whom compensation has been voted, is obliged to take it.

I think the Constitution intended to declare his right to it, and to make it obligatory upon Congress to ascertain the amount, and provide for its payment by law. That being done, the member might waive his constitutional right to receive it.

Since the public mind has been so greatly exercised on the subject, I have been painfully anxious to avail myself of all sources of information to furnish a guide to my action, particularly on the subject of "back pay." You will pardon me for asking you to travel with me through some of the stages of my investigation—bearing in mind that I am not hunting up apologies for a bad law, but only seeking light for my own action.

CONSTITUTIONALITY OF THE LAW.

I find, from examination of approved commentators, that the Constitution entrusted Congress with unlimited discretion over the subject of Congressional salaries. There was no check on the abuse of this discretion, except the terror and gibbet of public opinion. (1 Story on Constitution, section 358. See also Rawle and Kent on same subject.) But it has been conceded on all hands that the law, so far as the Congressional salary is concerned, is constitutional.

LEGISLATIVE ACTION.

I find that Congress inserted a back pay provision in the first salary bill of 1789, relating to the first of the term. As this was the first Congress, the back pay provision would not have great force as a precedent, as it might have been the result of necessity.

I find that the act passed March 19, 1816, contained a provision for back pay, and increased the compensation of members from the daily pay of $6, to the yearly pay of $1,500.

I find that the act of August 16, 1856, increased the compensation from a daily pay of $8, to a yearly pay of $3,000, containing a provision for back pay from the 4th of March, 1855, nearly eighteen months.

I find that the act of July 28, 1866, increased the pay from $3,000 to $5,000 per annum, to be "computed from the first day" of that Congress, which commenced on the 4th of March, 1865, nearly sixteen months.

PRESIDENTIAL ACTION.

I find that George Washington approved the Congressional compensation bill of 1789; Mr. Madison approved the act of 19th March, 1816; Mr. Pierce approved the act of 16th August, 1856; and Mr. Johnson approved the act of 26th July, 1866, which last act was passed by the vote: yeas 51, nays 50, not voting 85.

It is proper to state that none of these acts increased the compensation of the President.

REPRESENTATIVE STATESMEN.

I find that Henry Clay, though Speaker of the House at the time, took the floor and advocated the bill of 1816; and amongst others, the following representative statesmen voted for it: John C. Calhoun, Richard M. Johnson, James Clark, Benjamin Hardin, John McLean, Timothy Pickering, John Randolph, and Daniel Webster.

From the best information which I can obtain, all the Senators and Representatives of Congress at the time received the back pay under the act of 1856; amongst the distinguished Senators so receiving it were: James A. Bayard and John M. Clayton, of Delaware; John J. Crittenden, of Kentucky; Stephen A. Douglas and Lyman Trumbull, of Illinois; Lewis Cass, of Michigan; Samuel Houston, of Texas; James C. Jones and John Bell, of Tennessee.

All the Senators and Representatives in Congress at the time received the back pay under the act of 1866; amongst the distinguished statesmen were: T. A. Hendricks, of Indiana; Garret Davis and James Guthrie, of Kentucky; Reverdy Johnson, of Maryland; Henry Wilson and Charles Sumner, of Massachusetts; George H. Williams, of Oregon, now Attorney-general of the United States; and amongst these might be named all the delegation in the House from Tennessee. Rumor says that one Representative did not receive the back pay, but I have no authentic information of the fact.

ACTION OF THE PEOPLE.

The people expressed great indignation on the passage of the compensation act of 1816. Their clamor was so fierce that it forced a repeal of the act the next session of Congress. Mr. Mills, of Massachusetts, speaking on the question of the repeal of the law expressed the objection of the people fairly to it. "He had scarcely heard an intelligent man out of the House question the propriety of increasing the compensation. Such men had confined their complaints to the mode of increase, and that the law was retrospective in its operation, so that those who raised the compensation participated in the benefit of its increase, as well for that part of the session which had elapsed, as well for that which was to come." Mr. Clay had anticipated the objections of the people as to the propriety of members fixing their own compensation, and said: "As to the amendment to defer its operation until the next Congress, he would remark that, in his judgment, there was more propriety in the law ending than beginning there. It was more respectful to our successors to leave them free to determine what was the just measure of indemnity for their expenses, than for us to prescribe the rule for them. We can best judge for ourselves. With respect to the supposed delicacy of our fixing upon our own compensation, let the Constitution, let the necessity of the case be reproached for that, not us."

Mr. Randolph offered an amendment to the bill proposing to repeal the act of 1816, to deduct the back pay of members in excess of $6 per day, but it was rejected.

The people defeated some and re-elected others

who had aided in the passage of the law, The people, however, afterwards repeatedly honored Mr. Clay with their confidence, and a great national party gave him a most enthusiastic support as a candidate for the Presidency. Mr. Calhoun afterwards became Senator, Cabinet officer, and was elected Vice-President by the people. Mr. R. M. Johnson, author of the bill of 1816, was afterwards elected Vice-President by the people. Mr. McLean was afterwards made one of the Supreme Judges, and he was warmly solicited to become a candidate for the Presidency in 1832, but he declined. Mr. Webster was afterwards repeatedly in the Senate, in the Cabinet, supported by many warm friends as a candidate for the Presidency, and became illustrious as the greatest constitutional expounder of his age. James Clark was afterwards elected Governor of Kentucky. To single out a few who receivcd back pay under the act of 1856: Stephen A. Douglas and John Bell were endorsed by their respective parties as candidates for the Presidency when the times were "big with danger." John Bell carried the State of Tennessee. Lewis Cass afterwards became a Cabinet officer, and Lyman Trumbull and John J. Crittenden were sent to the Senate.

To single out a few who received back pay under the act of 1866: The eye of a great political party has been resting on T. A. Hendricks as a "coming man" for the high honors of the nation, Henry Wilson has been elected Vice-President by the Republican party, and many distinguished Representatives who received the back pay of both parties have been re-elected to Congress—such men as Eldridge, W. E. Niblack, M. C. Kerr, Samuel J. Randall,

Kelley, and Farnsworth; Randall not only having been re-elected to Congress, but made Chairman of the National Democratic Committee.

Franklin Pierce, after approving the compensation bill of 1856, received the vote of the delegates from Tennessee in the National Democratic Convention for renomination as a candidate for the Presidency.

And Mr. Johnson, after his approving the compensation bill of 1866, received strong legislative and popular support.

After this review, finding that the back pay feature of the different compensation laws have had the constitutional sanction, the legislative sanction, the Presidential sanction, the sanction of our great representative statesmen, and acquiescence, if not the sanction, of the people, candor compels me to admit, however much I might condemn the policy, that the recipients of the back pay have not been regarded as felons; and if the people so regarded them while their passion was so raging, they changed their opinion when they cooled down to the "second sober thought."

If the law had been unconstitutional, and Congress had knowingly and corruptly used the form of law to plunder the treasury, then those who participated in the plunder, whether voting for or against the bill, would be alike guilty. But if the law, on the other hand, was constitutional, as it certainly was, then it vested all the members voting for and against it with the legal right to the compensation, just as much as if the law were a grant of land or an appropriation of money for any other purpose.

Then, if vested with a title to it, the sequiter is inevitable that he has the right to receive it.

The act of drawing the money precedes and implies the power of disposing of it. Should any member fail to draw his back pay, it will remain to his credit "two years after the expiration of the fiscal year in which the act shall have been passed"—that is, from the 30th of June, 1874, the end of the fiscal year, to the 30th June, 1876, when it would lapse into the "surplus fund" of the treasury, and there to remain "without further and specific appropriation by law." This is upon the supposition that the salaries of members were liable to lapse under the law, which may be doubted. Assuming, however, that they do lapse, then they may be drawn at any time before the 30th of June, 1876. If any member should die before the expiration of the time, his personal representative might draw it within the remaining time. So, that if the member would give it back to the Government, or make any other disposition of it, he must draw it, or go through the form of drawing it.

But the most embarrassing question with which I have to deal, is:

WHAT WILL I DO WITH IT?

Various friends, with whom I have consulted, by no means agree as to what should be done with it. Some thought that it ought to be given back to the Government; others, that it ought to be turned over to the State of Tennessee; others, that it ought to be divided amongst the counties of my Congressional District; others, that I should keep it, as it was mine by the law of the land, and nothing but a fair compensation; others, that they would rather that I should have it than any other person, and that it would be unjust and unequal to take it from me when nearly all the other members kept theirs; and from abroad, it was solicited as a contribution to the Washington monument fund. So that it will be seen that the public mind has been at sea as well as my own.

If I should give it back to the Government, a certain class would cry out, with the New York Tribune, as it said of the back payers, that they "have been led by conscience, or driven by shame, or induced, by considerations of policy, to return it."

If I should propose to give it to the endowment fund of a university, the clamor comes from another quarter that I want to make it a sounding board of a mock liberality, which is only "charity in the rind, but selfishness in the core."

If I had left it in the treasury, the charge would have been made that it was only there with the dishonest motive of stealing it out after the storm had blown over.

If I propose to give it to the counties of my Congressional District, they are to be persuaded that the receipt of it would be contaminating.

If I propose to keep it, others raise the cry that I am guilty upon the principle that "the receiver is guilty as the thief."

If I refuse to speak out, I am considered dumb with conscious guilt. If I attempt an explanation, it is considered a hollow pretence, and like dog Tray, I must be beaten anyhow. So that I am held at bay on every side.

To give the money back, it would be only as the dust in the balances to the Government, whose annual expenses verge on $400,000,000. To give it to the State, or common school fund of the State, would not be just and equal to my own Congressional district, as the other Congressional Districts are receiving the benefit, in some form, of the quotas of their respective representatives.

But, fellow-citizens, not to weary you with further details: without your fault or mine, and over my opposition, we were involved in the consequences of the law, you by having your part of the increased salary to pay, I by being subjected to its burdens.

This last remark requires explanation: The larger the salary, the greater the exactions will be upon it. Washington City takes the gauge of the Congressional salary, and the price of rents, furniture, boarding, and provisions are raised in proportion to its increase.

Furnished houses, after the adjournment, could be rented for half the price exacted from the members during the session of Congress. The increased pay will only multiply the number and stimulate the importunity of demands upon it.

Congress is canvassed nearly every day for donations to charity indigence, and for contributions to religious, educational, literary, and scientific enterprises.

Besides, it is understood that a Congressman's salary is partly to be expended for the benefit of the public. He has to pay for all the printed copies of his own and other members' speeches, which he distributes amongst his constituents. He now has to pay postage on all the public documents, which he distributes, as well as letter postage to his constituents. He has to respond to the calls of his party to pay for the printing and distribution of canvass documents. He is expected to furnish relief to any of his constituents, or citizens of his State, who may happen to be caught in Washington City in a destitute condition. In short, he is tapped at every pore for money plethora, is expected to be as liberal as a prince; and if he withholds, he is berated as a niggard. Of all which I do not complain; I only state facts. Withal, he is expected, and it is his duty, to be an example of economy; and while he may be generous with his own, he must be saving of the public treasury.

I believe that the true theory of compensation to members of Congress was not designed to be in the extremes either of penury or prodigality; but, as said by one of the fathers of the Republic, it should be fixed "in the middle ground where dignity blends with economy."

In fact, it makes but little difference to the member of Congress whether his compensation be $5,000 and mileage, stationery, and free postage, or $7,500 without them. With either salary, the general average of the members will not more than make their ends meet.

Mr. Clay's experience was, that he could save no more out of the Speaker's salary—which was double that of other members—than he did out of his salary as a member on the floor.

However, it is a matter of difference to the people who have the increased compensation to pay. Perhaps, it is the duty of members of Congress to wage a war of economy upon the exactions incident to Congressional life.

After this explanatory digression on the supervening burdens of the salary, I recur to the train of thought on which I was commenting: that you and myself were involved in the consequences of the law, without the fault of either. You have your quota to pay. It is beyond the power of Congress to compel a restitution, at least as to the outgoing members, and it could reach the present members only by deducting the back pay from their future compensation.

From the foregoing review to throw light on my own action, I conclude that by the sanction of the Constitution of the United States—by the sanction of the official antecedents of Presidents and representative statesmen of the purest days of the Republic, the back pay is mine.

I did not expect it, did not ask it, did not vote for it. The Government has parted with it, has no claim on it, does not ask its return. Being mine, I may do with it as I please. My constituents having had it to pay, are the only persons on earth who can raise the question of a primary equity. The imperious logic of facts drives me to this conclusion.

Being mine, I had intended, and privately so expressed my intention, to offer it in pro rata proportions to the counties composing the 4th Congressional District, (and which district I was proud to represent), through their County Courts; not because I had stolen it; not because I was conscious-stung, like Judas, to cast it at your feet as the fee of treachery; for I did not betray you.

Nor did I intend to offer it as a bribe for any future preferment, nor use it as a screen to anticipated resentment. I felt as jealous of your honor as of my own, and I would have scorned to propose any thing which I thought indefensible in law or morals.

Recent circumstances, however, have induced me to change my intentions. I decline now to make the offer to the County Courts, for the reason that an effort has been made to forestal their impartial action, and because such offers elsewhere have been decried and rejected as the specious overtures of the demagogue. Popular jealousy is so aroused that I am put to a disadvantage on all sides.

I understand my embarrassing posture. If I should make the offer, an effort would be made to have it rejected with insult; if I do not make the offer, I may be snubbed for the refusal.

As their representative, I claim that I am entitled to the fair and impartial judgment of the people. First know, next deliberate, and then judge.

Notwithstanding I decline a tender to the County Courts, yet if the people in any or all of the counties in the Congressional District, assert a primary equity to the back pay by any general expression, in deference to their wish, I will take pleasure in sending such county a check for its pro rata share, on application of a proper agent to receive it.

Accepting an advantage under an unwise and impolitic law, by no means commits us to an endorsement of it.

Many of our purest and best citizens have taken stock in our National Banks who were opposed to the whole banking system, and would have voted against the law authorizing them had they been members of Congress. They availed themselves of their advantages because they were lawful, although the avowed object of their creation was to break down the banking institutions of the States and centralize the banking powers of the nation in the General Government. At the same time, all the people became involved in the consequences by being compelled to use the currency.

I do not claim that my legislative action is above criticism. To expect infallibility of me would be to measure me by a standard by which none of you would be willing to be measured.

You may acquit me of sordid motives when I tell you that I voted for the repeal of the franking privilege, the effect of which was to relieve the Government from paying, as to myself, from $300 to $500 per year, and to impose the burden upon my salary when it stood at $5,000 per year, with no prospect of increasing it at the time. I thought the franking privilege right within itself, but it was asserted that the privilege had been greatly abused during the last Presidential canvass, as well as at other times, and I yielded up my private advantage to correct a public abuse.

I voted against the salary bill to defeat it when it was known that its defeat would result in a called session of Congress, which would enhance my personal expenses.

It was a bad law, and I rejoice to know that I represented you in voting against it. You stand right, through your representative, on the record.

You had cause to arouse your alarm at the rapid drift of the Government to extravagance. In 1856, the Congressional salary had been increased from $8 per day to $3,000 per year with mileage; in 1866, it was increased to $5,000 per year with mileage and stationery; in 1873, it was increased to $7,500 with actual traveling expenses, less mileage and stationery, at the same time increasing the salaries of numerous other officers of the Government, and at a time when there was no financial crisis, when there was no blight of the harvests, nor disease of the flocks and herds to raise the cost of living to famine prices, and at a time when the people were galled and staggering under the burden of taxation, my voice has been lifted against subsidies, monopolies, and exorbitant taxation.

It has been my highest ambition, by faithful service, to win your approbation, which is the true reward of the patriot.

JOHN M. BRIGHT.

FAYETTEVILLE, TENN.

www.ingramcontent.com/pod-product-compliance
Lightning Source LLC
LaVergne TN
LVHW011141110826
845150LV00008B/2441

* 9 7 8 1 4 1 8 1 9 2 7 0 9 *